Perspectives
The Impact of Climate Change
Why Clean Energy Matters

Series Consultant: Linda Hoyt

Flying Start
to Literacy®

Contents

Our changing climate: who are the victims?

The world is getting warmer and it is changing our climate. That's the latest report from the United Nation's panel of scientific experts – the Intergovernmental Panel on Climate Change (IPCC).

To avoid dangerous climate change, the IPCC says the unrestricted use of fossil fuels as a source of energy has to be phased out. When we make and use energy from fossil fuels, dangerous gases can be released into the air. These gases have made our world warmer. They are changing the climate and having a drastic effect on communities all around the world.

What can we do to help?

Kids fight for the environment

A group of 21 young activists aged 9 to 20 have filed a lawsuit in the United States claiming that the United States government has failed to control carbon emissions, and that this violates the rights of young people all over the country. They're asking the court to require the government to come up with a bold plan to halt global warming.

The people suing, or plaintiffs, point out that climate change isn't just something that might hurt them in the future — it's affecting them right now.

What concerns do you have about global warming and climate change?

The plaintiffs

Alex

"I grew up on my family's farm along a river. Climate change-related drought, disease, and changes in predator and insect activity are threatening the elk and wild turkeys that my family and I hunt for food.

Wildfires are growing more common, and the smoke has made my asthma worse. High temperatures are damaging our farm's hazelnut trees. I'm afraid the farm won't survive the changing climate."

Xiuhtezcatl

"I live in Boulder, Colorado, in the United States. I visit nearby forests not only for recreation, but also to participate in the ceremonies and dances that are part of my family's Aztec heritage. However, wildfires and infestations of mountain pine beetles (which thrive in heat) make it harder for me to spend time in the forest."

Jaime

"I grew up on the Navajo Nation Reservation in Arizona in the United States. As a child, I helped my mother with farming and tending animals. But the springs on the reservation dried up. Hauling water for our family and our animals was so expensive that we could no longer make a living, so we had to leave our home.

Away from the reservation, I have fewer chances to participate in traditional Navajo ceremonies. I worry that even my new home may not be safe, as forest fires recently forced my family to evacuate for two days."

Xiuhtezcatl Martinez leads a youth rally against fracking in Denver, Colorado.

Jayden

"My family has experienced three hurricanes since moving to Louisiana in the United States. We lost power and water for a week during one hurricane."

Victoria

"I live in White Plains, in the state of New York in the United States. We lost power and saw schools and public transportation shut down after Hurricane Sandy in 2012."

Miko

"I live in Oregon in the United States, but I was born in the Marshall Islands, a country in the Pacific Ocean between Hawaii and Australia. I'm worried I'll never be able to return there because rising sea levels may one day submerge the islands."

In conclusion

Though climate change is likely not the only reason for every one of the environmental changes these young people are experiencing, it definitely seems to be a contributing factor.

Kids vs. government

In November 2016, the 21 young activists won a big victory when a federal judge ruled that the lawsuit they had filed against the United States government could go forward. Writer and former lawyer Alice Andre-Clark explains the lawsuit.

Do you agree with what these young people are doing? It is very possible that they will lose. Do you think it is worth the fight? Are there other ways that you could get your views heard?

Twenty-one young activists, working with lawyers at Our Children's Trust, state that the government has known for decades that fossil fuel emissions are causing the climate to change. Nevertheless, it has allowed businesses to drill for fossil fuels, to burn them and to transport them around the country.

The young people argue that the policies that have led to climate change violate their right of due process. Under the 5th Amendment to the US Constitution, government may not take away your life, liberty or property without going through a decision-making process that considers your rights fairly.

The young people say that the government is violating their rights by endangering their health and making it hard for them to acquire food, enjoy clean air and water, live in safe homes and practise their religions.

The young people claim that by allowing activities that contribute to climate change, the government also violates their right to equal protection. The 14th Amendment to the US Constitution says that government can't make laws that treat one group of people differently from another without a legal process.

The young people argue that by indirectly contributing to climate change, the government has treated young people and future generations unfairly compared to the current generation of adults who grew up in a safer climate, and who now make money from drilling for and burning fossil fuels.

People around the world are calling for climate justice. These protesters live on an island in Bangladesh that has been affected by rising tides and intense storms.

It's a tough fight, but if these young activists win, the effect on the environment could be significant. They're asking the court to declare that the government's failure to stop climate change violates Americans' constitutional rights.

In November 2016, they celebrated a victory when a federal judge ruled that the lawsuit could go forward. She reviewed their legal documents and found that they'd stated strong claims that the government's failure to address climate change had violated their rights.

Next, the young people and their lawyers will work to prove their case at trial.

Fleeing from the weather

"Refugee" usually describes someone who is forced to flee from his or her own country and seek safety somewhere else because of political issues such as war or genocide, religion or race.

But did you know that there are climate refugees? In this article, Marcia Amidon Lusted tells us about the growing number of people who are forced to leave their homes because of changes in the weather.

How would you feel if this happened to you?

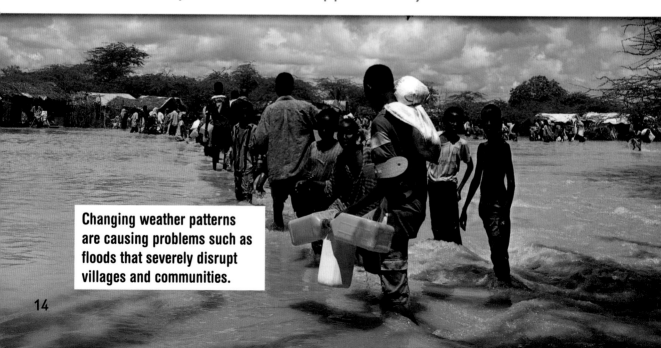

Changing weather patterns are causing problems such as floods that severely disrupt villages and communities.

A climate refugee is someone who is forced to leave home because of sudden or long-term changes to their environment created by climate change. These changes include droughts, flooding from excessive rain, rising sea levels, desertification and changes in the normal weather patterns, including more frequent extreme weather events such as cyclones and monsoons.

Years of drought have affected many parts of Africa.

These changes can drastically affect a family's ability to survive. It makes it difficult for them to grow food, find clean water and make a living. Many climate scientists are predicting a rise in global temperatures and higher sea levels that will continue over the next 100 years. If that is true, the problem of climate refugees will only increase.

According to the International Red Cross and Red Crescent health organisations, more people are now forced to leave their homes because of environmental disasters than because of war. And more than half of the world's refugees could actually be classified as climate refugees. By 2050, there could be as many as 150 million climate refugees.

Many places in the world have already seen changes that are forcing people to leave their countries and become refugees.

Rising sea levels in the Pacific Ocean

Many people who live on islands in the Pacific Ocean have seen their crops and gardens washed away or the soil contaminated by the salt of rising seawater levels. In addition, they no longer catch as many fish because rising ocean temperatures are bleaching coral reefs and depleting the fish population.

These islands also experience water shortages during droughts or sudden torrents of rain during tropical storms due to changing rainfall patterns.

Family members gather rocks and corals from the seabed to build a stone wall as protection against rising sea levels in Kiribati.

People from drought-affected Somalia wait to get water at a refugee camp.

Droughts in Africa

In other parts of the world there is not enough water due to changing weather patterns. Years of drought have affected millions of people in Africa. The group Save the Children estimates that every day 800 children cross the border into Kenya from Somalia.

Children and adults in Somalia are suffering from malnutrition because crops have failed and livestock are dying. The United Nations has even called the current Somali drought the worst humanitarian disaster in the world. And yet Kenya cannot handle the number of climate refugees streaming in from Somalia. Refugee camps are overflowing and there is a desperate need for food and other supplies.

17

Hurricanes in the United States

In the United States, the devastation caused by Hurricane Katrina in New Orleans in 2005 resulted in many people losing their homes, their businesses and their jobs. As a result, many people were evacuated to other parts of the country, and many of them settled in those places permanently. With no jobs or homes available to them in their own city, they became climate refugees within their own country because of the storm. Hurricane Sandy, which hit the east coast of the United States in 2012, also caused widespread destruction.

Thousands of people were left homeless after Hurricane Katrina blew through New Orleans, Louisiana on 30 August 2005.

What can we do about climate refugees?

For those who have been forced to flee because of climate change, it might be impossible for them to ever go home. There is widespread agreement that the lag time for the reduction in gas and oil emissions to take effect is 100 years or more. So climate refugees won't be going back to their homes, but perhaps future generations may.

Scientists are working on methods that may allow crops to grow despite our changing environment. Countries that are less affected by climate and weather disasters could provide more aid (both money and supplies) to countries where there are people suffering from environmental catastrophes.

Unfortunately, it's a problem that's only going to grow in the years to come, and now is the best time for people – and especially young people – to start thinking about the world as a global community, where everyone depends on and helps everyone else.

If we think of ourselves as a world without borders, then climate refugees will no longer be refugees. They'll just be neighbours in need.

Eyes on the tide

Many Pacific Island nations are facing destruction from rising sea levels. In this article, Judy Walker explains the problem faced by Pacific Islanders as the sea level rises and threatens their homes.

What would you do if your town began to sink under the waves? Whose problem is it? Should the rest of the world help out? What do you think?

Rising tides

The Pacific Ocean covers almost a third of the Earth. Scattered around its rim are many groups of islands. In recent years, the people of these islands have noticed tides getting higher and storms getting worse. And they wonder – is their world about to change?

As the climate warms, the huge ice sheets at the North and South Poles are melting, releasing water into the oceans. That makes the oceans higher, like when you add water to a bath. Warmer water also takes up a bit more room than cooler water, so as the oceans warm they rise even more. Scientists expect that if the planet continues to warm, sea levels around the world may rise 30 to 120 centimetres or more by 2100. That may not sound like much, but it's alarming news for islanders and anyone else who lives near the coast.

1.
Earth warms.

2.
Ice melts exposing land and ocean.

3.
Land and Ocean hold more heat.

4.
Sea levels rise. Land disappears.

5.
Flooding is more frequent.

6.
Drinking water becomes polluted.

Island life

The Solomon Islands are a group of 1000 small islands in the South Pacific. Five of the islands have disappeared beneath the waves since 1947. At high tide, water flows into houses and over roads that used to be dry. As the sea levels rise, salt water seeps up through the ground, getting into wells and killing trees and crops.

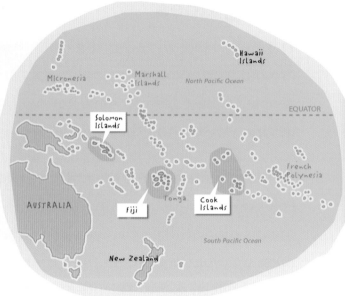

The people of the Solomon Islands are working with scientists to build seawalls to protect homes from rising water and storms. They're trying to cut down fewer trees, since trees help hold onto soil. They're growing crops in containers to keep the salt water out, or finding crops that don't mind salt. They're planting mangrove trees and corals to protect the coasts. They hope that by working hard, they can find a way to stay on their islands – at least for a while.

One village on the island of Vanua Levu in Fiji decided on a drastic solution when their homes started flooding every time the tide came in – they moved the whole town up into the hills. They built new houses, dug fish ponds and started growing pineapples. Some miss their old life by the sea – but at least they're safe, and still together.

Whose problem?

All these solutions – building seawalls, storing water, moving a town – cost money. Some island nations would like the rest of the world to help them deal with the problems caused by climate change or help them find new homes. After all, they argue, the planet is warming because people all over the world are burning fossil fuels.

Pacific Islanders make very little of this pollution, but they're suffering a lot from the effects. If cars and factories in America, Europe, Asia and Australia cause floods on the other side of the world, whose problem is it? Maybe we can take a lesson from the oceans. Melting ice in the Arctic makes higher waves in Fiji because all the oceans are connected. When there are changes in one place, the changes affect other places. Change one, change all. If we're going to fix the problems of climate change, maybe the world will have to work together as one.

What is your opinion?: How to write a persuasive argument

1. State your opinion

Think about the issues related to your topic. What is your opinion?

2. Research

Research the information you need to support your opinion.

Related PERSPECTIVES book   Internet   Other sources

3. Make a plan

Introduction

How will you "hook" the reader?

State your opinion.

List reasons to support your opinion.

What persuasive devices will you use?

Reason 1
Support your reason with evidence and details.

Reason 2
Support your reason with evidence and details.

Reason 3
Support your reason with evidence and details.

Conclusion

Restate your opinion. Leave your reader with a strong message.

4. Publish

Publish your persuasive argument.

Use visuals to reinforce your opinion.